MORE THAN A CEASE FIRE

(in 100 Haikus)

poems by
Amy Cronin DiCaprio

MORE THAN A CEASE FIRE

Copyright © 2020 by Amy Cronin DiCaprio
All rights reserved.
ISBN 9798583274154

"We are not idealized wild things.
We are imperfect mortal beings,
aware of that mortality even as we push it away,
failed by our very complication,
so wired that when we mourn our losses
we also mourn, for better or for worse, ourselves.
As we were. As we are no longer.
As we will one day not be at all"

- Joan Didion, *The Year of Magical Thinking*

CONTENTS

WILD LIFE	7
THE BEECH TREE GREW	9
MADE A FOOL OF BY THE MACAWS, WHO MATED FOR LIFE	11
IL N'EXISTE PLUS	13
IT WAS A WOLF	15
A DOUBLE EDGED SWORD	16
ROUTES (63)	17
MAKE IT DARK, MAMA	19
UP IN FLAMES	21
THAT DON'T MAKE IT JUNK	22
TWIN HIGH MAINTENANCE MACHINES	23
THE MIRAGE OF IT	25
THE IMPERFECT PAST	26

WILD LIFE

There is only one
photo I love of myself:
You caught me, off guard

in bed, windows flung
wide open, a double bed
on Rue Saint-Denis,

metal balcony
in the 4th arrondissement.
Brand new and in love

as we searched the streets
for that one fromagerie
you'd found the first day

Reading Dutch menus
in Amsterdam - *what a dream,*
                    Van Gogh museum...

My own appetite
thrilled me: a summer buffet
         Oregon blue cheese

                    West-coast IPA's
                         the Ukiah hospital
                              Pink Panther sweatpants

In our blue bedroom,
one night when I couldn't sleep,
you held me, said to

> imagine that the
> traffic outside was the waves
> on Luquillo Beach

THE BEECH TREE GREW

One night before bed
I slid on my wedding ring
to see how it felt;

to see if i'd sleep.
    In my dream, a cardinal
    flew into the house,

        so taut and cautious,
        and more than red; charcoal tips
        on his wings, his eyes

        almost blue, opaque.
        He crouched in the fruit bowl, with
        the avocados

        until i opened
        the back door, grabbed the red broom
        and shooed him outside

like you'd told me to
on South Street when our cat caught
a blackbird at dawn.

I did it right; my
vision narrowed to the task
at hand, and he flew

straight to the beech tree
which now fills the whole frame
of the kitchen window.

>An apology
>In my mouth when I wake up;
>fatigue, like dry hands

>on my scalp, prodding
>me to face the future- and
>then - to face the past.

I looked for him while
the french press sat brewing and
then I remembered

that I hadn't seen
him all autumn or winter:
>did he leave with you?

MADE A FOOL OF BY THE MACAWS, WHO MATED FOR LIFE

I wanted to be
the sky: bright blue and shameless,
Instead, I was stuck

like the green front door
when it swelled in its frame and
refused to open.

The cause mattered less
than the effect, in the end,
eclipsing itself

I had been hungry
hunger makes a sandwich good.
       and then the story

       changes like moonstones
and my self interest curdles -
and turns on itself...

...inside me, something
stumbles to the edge of a
precipice; falls off.

IL N'EXISTE PLUS

When you signed your lease,
I took the tomato knife
to the cedar chest

and pried off the plaque
    Uncle Russel had made, our
    wedding date engraved

    so 'you'd remember'
    (when I'm the one who forgot)
dragged the brass corner

across my forearm
drawing a thin line of blood
to manage the pain

the room is haunted
invisible ink, scrawling,
on our bedroom walls.

Cut open the years
before 'This Happened' -- they'd be
riddled with disease-

passing the batons
of chaos and resentment,
tamping down desire,

the monotonous
loops of domesticity.
You are no Hugo,

and I should say, too,
I am no Pussywillow.
But what good was I

while the wheels turned slow:
circling each other - wary,
betrayed and longing.

IT WAS A WOLF

I waited for you,
but I see now: I never
told you where I was.

Nothing can quite make
you feel invisible like
being a liar

A girl who cries wolf:
sounding alarms, desperate,
and hiding her face

But there is no wolf.
She's seen herself, abhorrent:
lies, "It was a wolf."

A DOUBLE-EDGED SWORD

I loved our date nights-
they felt like another world.
You would pour the wine--

the grease for the wheels
that turned us, rounding corners,
towards each other.

Turns out that twelve years
of drinking for free can be
a double-edged sword

the pleasure of a
well-made key sliding into
place, turning just right,

how the screws that keep
me tightened with shame and rage
loosen half a turn.

A mobius strip
      (no boundaries, and one-sided)
of pain, and relief.

ROUTES (63)

I could drive this road
with my eyes shut-- go sailing
around curves my arms

memorized sixteen
years ago: the golden hours
of the golden age

Grey '87
Plymouth Reliant with no
    air conditioning

        roll-down windows fogged
        on New Year's Eve as we drove
        for Chinese take-out

Our first rental car:
    me hyperventilating
    an hour past Big Sur...

Years later, pregnant,
    the bumps on Bay Road that gave
    me false contractions

and later still, both
>   kids asleep in the backseat;
>   we blasted Tom Waits
>
>   driving home, late, from
>   New York: when we were faded
>   but still hanging on,
>
>   singing, to ourselves,
>   *You Can Never Hold Back Spring*
>   praying ragged prayers

And the darkest year:
>   I drove my dream car straight through
>   a telephone pole.
>
>   I'm still not sure I
>   didn't die. Dwindling half lives
>   of our memories
>
>   kicking the back of
>   my seat when I drive. And I
>   take the long way home.

MAKE IT DARK, MAMA

Most nights I dream of
salt water, and of small skiffs
that aren't seaworthy.

The past is a tide,
waves of backbreaking wreckage
sucking me under

all the way under,
down to the rich bottom mud,
the metallic cold.

And in the morning
I can't tell which way is up.
My sons fish me out

when they come wake me.
The weightlessness of water
bleeds into the day

and I stay adrift.
Some mornings, I keep them there
in the bed with me

under the covers,
half-resting, and half-trampled,
hiding, but still seen.

    "Make it dark, Mama."
"Look: you can make it yourself:
just cover your eyes

with your own two hands"
    *"Ta-da! I'm invisible!
    Can you still see me?"*

He says he wishes
his superpower was to
be invisible

I say mine would be
to stop time.   *"What would you do
    in the time, Mama?"*

In his hand is a
stray hairpin he found under
my pillow, and he

is making it dance,
absentminded, his wild hair
soft under my chin

    "To do what, Mama?"
I consider his question.
"Be awake with you."

UP IN FLAMES

If you could have known:
would you still have given me
the tomato knife?

the solstice chaos-
tissue paper up in flames-
a freshwater pearl

on the wrong finger,
my back up against the fridge,
reeling, kissing you.

The blue formica.
The yellow linoleum.
I had everything.

THAT DON'T MAKE IT JUNK

I cleaned the garage
nine months after you'd moved out
and I found a card

I'd written you: your
name, drawn in a heart on the
envelope, which was

now full of spiders--
you'd left it in the garage
for years, forgotten,

rotting under the
hornet spray and turpentine.
You never liked notes.

TWIN HIGH MAINTENANCE MACHINES

My first dream of us
was a nightmare. I dreamt it
over and over.

It would start the same:
your green Ford sedan, losing
control, and skidding

in the gravel of
a hair-pin turn. Your face young;
-younger than you were-

and we would fly right
off a cliff, suffocating
in sick dream silence.

The first time, we cried,
wordlessly. The second time,
screamed at each other,

belligerent, and
desperate, before crashing
into the rocks. Once,

we clawed at the doors,
at the locks and the windows:
but where could we go?

The last one: we locked
eyes and held hands, so resigned.
I want a new dream.

THE MIRAGE OF IT

A pin-dot of hope -
family dinners, all of us,
four plates and four forks

tender and raw from
where we licked our exit wounds:
new layers of skin -

scar-strewn and shiny
pink - I pull my sweater sleeves
down, over dry fists,

then push them back up,
force my shaking hands to keep
threading the needle

to try and repair
what frayed; neglected, before
I gave up: tore it.

I would get a dog.
I forget the question but
the answer is you.

THE IMPERFECT PAST

"The imperfect past"
...my favorite tense... the hope of
unfinished actions...

Progressive tenses
(in English) are imperfect
And wonderfully so...

...unflinchingly so...
the repeatability
is what defines them

"I loved you so much."
Compared with this simple past:
"I loved you then."   And

that imperfect past:
It broke me and I broke us
        But that's   unfinished

Made in the USA
Middletown, DE
15 January 2021